Angel

on

Vacation

Nicholai Vytautus

My Fat Fox

MMXIV

My Fat Fox Ltd

86 Gladys Dimson House

London E7 9DF

United Kingdom

www.myfatfox.co.uk

SECOND PAPERBACK EDITION

Angel On Vacation © 2007, 2014 by Nicholai Vytautus

The rights of Nicholai Vytautus to be identified as the author of this work have been asserted by him in accordance with the Copyright, Designs and Patents Act, 1988

Cover design by Hartmut Jager

http://hartmut–jager.artistwebsites.com/

ISBN 978-1-905747-27-6

There's connection and order,

love and guidance,

eternity and evolution

within the group creation

of all realities.

Contents

Introduction

In the late 1990s, my son and I took a two-day long train trip. During the ride he asked me to hypnotize him, as if he were a client. I believe it's unethical to hypnotize children, and he was only 12, so instead I taught him how to relax his body by gently "allowing" it to feel warm and heavy, progressively relaxing himself from his feet to his head. Then I asked him to just tell me about the pictures in his mind. The after-death communications researcher and co-author of *Hello Heaven!,* Bill Guggenheim, had suggested that if I ever work with children I should use this simple non-hypnotic technique.

I took notes as best I could, given that as a hypnotherapist I was used to taping sessions with clients as well as recording conversations by hand. When we arrived at my mother's home, we did another relaxing session during which my son answered questions I had about the first session, and he drew a few sketches in my notebook. We had two more short sessions after returning home; I recorded one of them. Listening now to us eleven years ago has been a great joy, especially knowing that these sessions were pivotal for both of us. I've attempted to put the notes together in a way that flows; they aren't necessarily chronological. Some parts have been rearranged according to their subject matter.

Up until this event my only child had been a forthright, caustic little Anarchist atheist, making fun of his church-going friends, wise-cracking at my alien-believing friends, and just having an all around iconoclastic good time at the expense of others' beliefs. I can't count how many times I heard, "His mouth will get him into trouble!"

It wasn't only his caustic mouth that caused trouble. When he was a bit older he 'mooned' the Special Needs bus driver. He drank alcohol and smoked cigarettes and grass. He left school before graduating the day he turned sixteen. And, at a solid 6'4", I heard he did his fair share of telling off bullies behind the movie house in town. He was also outstanding in baseball, hockey, and soccer. He had the lead part in a high school drama production. He was in a performing boy choir for 3 years, with a solo, and he was lead singer, and then drummer, in a few rock bands. My son loves life, and has an unusual depth of understanding, but no one, other than I, had any idea he was anything like an angel!

He became more thoughtful after the "sessions", even though he still acted like he was here to have fun. He remembers everything he recalled on the train, and more, but until now it hasn't been easy to get him to talk about it. He still thinks churchgoers are "sheep" but from our sessions he gained a solid belief in God, in Heaven and Hell in the Whiteness, and in the reality of aliens, angels, and an afterlife. He also found a deep reservoir of wisdom within himself which makes me feel honored to have brought this life into being.

The stories in this little book have changed my life. Having since specialized in investigative hypnosis, I'm delighted that they have consistency and hang together as a whole. When we took our train ride, I was new in the field; my questions would be more formal now but, perhaps, less interesting. My son's answers to my questions have given me a certainty about life and the afterlife that I didn't quite yet have, even after all of my own meetings with ghosts, and all of the many past life regressions I've done, and the years I've spent studying philosophy and theology.

For eleven years my son did not want me to share these stories with anyone. I suppose he was embarrassed. He's now ready to talk about them; he's happy to have me work on them, get them published, and talk about them. He would even be happy for us

3

to use our real names, but I prefer to be more cautious, and it was my decision to use a pseudonym. Perhaps this little book is one reason that Dick, the Carrier Angel, is here now.

If you, too, ask the children in your life to tell you about the pictures in their minds, I hope that you will be as richly rewarded as I was.

The Cathedral Near the End of Space

&

"It is Nothing and Everything"

Okay, now that you're relaxed, please tell me what you see.

I see marble, a church hallway, a Gothic cathedral.

The biggest door is made of wood; it's rough and old. I open it.

Something black ran out!

It's just a huge floating dark robe and it flies away.

Please, look down and describe what you see.

My sandals are made of cork.

My feet are covered with white light. They're white, middle-aged, not hairy; very clean.

I can't see my legs.

I'm wearing a white robe with a dark outline, not silk but like it, edged in black. It goes almost down to my feet and wraps down in front like an upside down "V".

Describe your hands.

> My hands are white; I have medium-long fingers, no jewelry - wait - a gold band on my left ring finger, but I'm not married.

Please, look around and describe what you see.

> I'm in space and behind me is a large church. It's huge! I came out of a small entrance, but behind it it's huge.

> There are cities and a castle; it has a beehive look. There's stained glass on the bottom in a smooth rock floor. The rock near the outside is smooth.

> There are little lights, like electric charges; making little jumps, little flashes; but they're stationary, on top of cones.

What are they?

> The lights are Glastonbury Places. They're very big.

Where are you?

> It won't let me tell you what it's called.

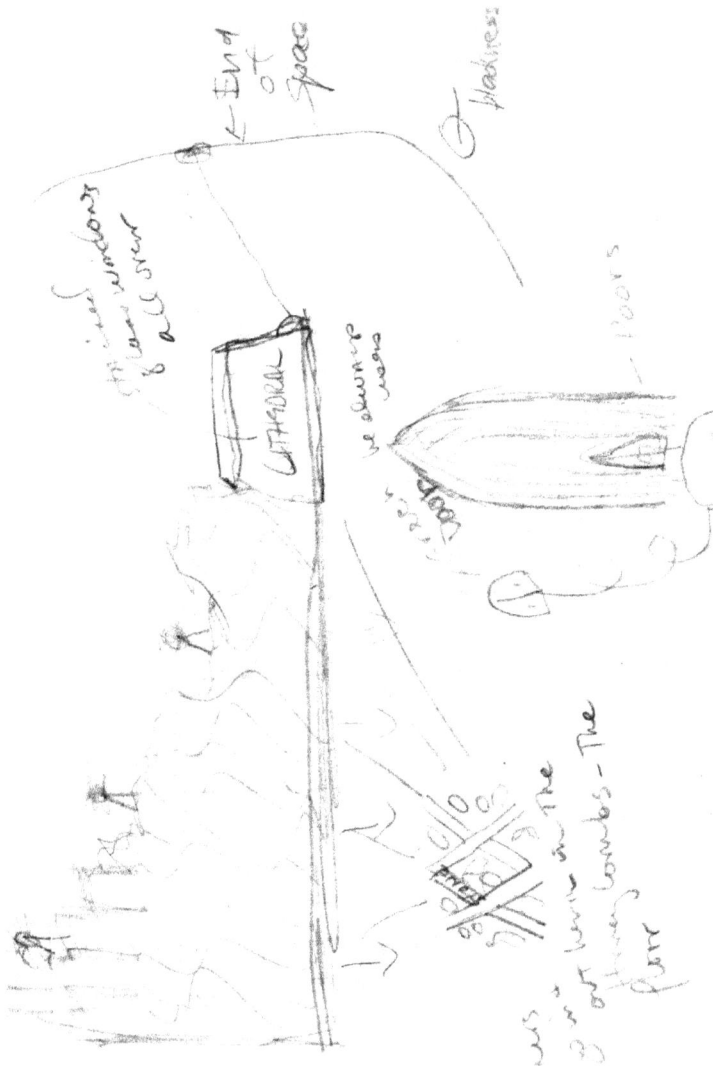

There's no other life here.

The beehive parts have stained glass
floors but don't walk on it!

This is where things enter and leave the Continuum. None stay.

This is near the End of Space.

There's an end to space?

There's so much that it seems an infinity, but it ends.

I've been there - I hit it - I laid up against it like a glass wall. You can't go through it.

The stars end. Nobody knows if anything's out there.

What were you doing there?

I was just flying around with my friends, looking for stuff.

Who are your friends?

My friends are like me, except one's fat and one's dark red with dark black hair, coarse like horsehair, short. He's kind of bald. He's Tahil. He always wears green; it's a classification.

What does green mean?

Green indicates responsibility, and white to help others.

We get days off to do other stuff like cruise to look for stuff.

Ron, Ronnie, Ronald. He seems to be... he's very plump and has an accent. He's wearing the same thing.

I've known them many transformations, many lives.

Where are they now?

They've stayed together. They've gone to a place I didn't want to go because I was sick of... it was a very unbeautiful place with lots of partying. They wanted to not always be so serious and to party.

I always wanted to be here because it's beautiful, but not as beautiful as before.

I like beautiful things. This life will be a good one.

[Bobo, the brown Siamese cat, checks what we're doing.]

Cats are elsewhere in the universe but they're not as loving. Cats here are pets; elsewhere they're wild hunters. They kill people and even other life forms that rule over other animals. Large packs, hundreds of them, attack.

We've taken them apart here and one-on-one they can do no harm.

Animals have and will rule here again.

Do you still have contact with your friends?

Sometimes I see them around when I'm traveling in my sleep. They come to visit me.

"We'll meet up with you again," they tell me.

My life here is but a blink out there; it's so quick, yet worth so much more because of the experience. This will train me for many other places I'll be going to.

I have to come to Earth on missions in the future; it's expected of me.

What's your name and what are your missions?

I'm Dick, and I'm sent by them. I just get a message. I see them in forms of energy. They come in front of you and tell you to do this or that.

They ask you to do something expected of you. You're not respected as much if you don't do it. You don't have to, but…

They work for It, The One. He is The One, but there's more over Him. He takes orders from others. No one knows who The Highest is, no one except The Big It. It is not life. It lives within another, or others.

There has been a God within us, sometimes, for help or in times of grief, but it's not always experienced by us.

There's a God over the Earth. Jesus is considered a God under The One. There are many.

What is a Lord?

A Lord is someone we ask upon for

things, and hope, and redemption, which they can relay to God or not.

There are Lords even though they're not called Lords; they may only be feelings. It's impossible for you to understand now, although you might someday.

You can go towards the center because you can't go away.

Center? What is there "out there"?

There's more than space; there's the Whiteness where everyone goes.

There's no Heaven or Hell, no good or bad place. When you're done with life here you go on to the Whiteness, and then on to other planets.

Hell is for the extremely bad, like if you kill thirty people you might have to spend time (which doesn't matter because you can experience three human months or six human years in six seconds) in a very horrible place. Whatever's hidden in your mind that you don't like will happen to you.

There's no punishment?

Yes, there is punishment, but it's hard to earn. It's for taking from others.

If you don't feel good about life you go to a place where you will be loved.

What is the Whiteness?

The Whiteness is whatever emotion you have for it.

Remember something important.

Others are here following expected jobs, too.

They're here to find out more about Earth, which is considered a beautiful planet except by the people who are destroying it.

Other planets have been destroyed; many through carelessness, by thinking of the planet as a place and not as something that should receive love as any other thing.

When did you first begin to exist?

I've always existed, just not always as

life.

The universe is still fairly new.

The mind is an infinity.

If used correctly your soul will take you anywhere.

The soul is not your heart, nor your little toe. It inhabits the body; it fits into the body.

It is nothing and everything; so huge and so small.

On Earth, soul is partially asleep.

We're not using all of the brain. Others are figuring out why we don't use it. They have to figure it out.

My soul is locked against telling. There are restrictions here. There are things everyone knows but cannot tell.

It's a small insignificant thing, the knowledge of what to do and how to do it to use our brains.

Our bodies are one of the most complex in the Continuum.

We can't unlock that knowledge because it would hurt us; we're not ready. We would make us destroy ourselves. So much knowledge; it wouldn't be peaceful now.

Why don't some of those here studying us tell us what to do?

They know not to tell us. They don't tell us enough; they just give us clues.

We don't use 89% of our brains.

The 11% we do use is nothing, yet we still enjoy life.

What do you do between missions?

Last time I hung out with friends. Stayed in the Whiteness, called on many friends and had fun; partied. But you get tired of that.

Life is like a school trip: it sucks, but it's kinda fun.

This life is somewhat of a vacation. It's simplicity!

There are no real threats other than

wrecking the planet.

We've brought so many problems on ourselves!

Small tribes, cities, nationalities, we've made so many problems we don't see the real problem: we're ruining our planet!

This is why we can't open up our brain. If we could this would be the most beautiful planet ever.

Why doesn't someone help us?

5,000 people know, maybe.

They're here to study why we haven't figured it out.

When we do figure it out we won't be on our own, but until then, we are.

World War II
Jewish-American Soldier

*N*ow, please tell me something else important to you that you see in your mind.

I see my house.

It has a nice looking rug.

There's a little old-fashioned radio.

It's just a house.

I'm a little baby boy, all alone in this room.

Why are you alone?

Oh, if I were to cry out someone would come.

I have a rattle but I'm looking around. I'm happy.

Now I'm in school. Listening to the radio. I'm 13 to 16 years old. Talking about the news, about Fascism.

What's the date?

It's June 13th, 1933.

What language are you speaking?

English.

I live in a town in Connecticut.

I'm beating the crap out of some kid - just fighting. I win. I feel good.

Now I'm home, looking at some books, and I see the word "Yorksburg". Must be the name of my school.

It's my graduation. My father, mother, little brother and little sister are here.

Now I see signs that say "Join the Army" so I join with a whole bunch of friends. I feel good since I'm with my friends.

I had army training for three months. Then I'm on a ship.

How old are you now?

20-23 years old.

Still a lot of talk about Fascism but I don't know what it means.

I just joined because of my friends.

I hear stuff about Jewish and Polish people, about cleansing; is this made up stuff to make others look bad?

I am Jewish.

I come from a rich family. We don't go to temple.

I went to a <u>lot</u> of parties when I was small; to a lot of places I didn't like with my family - sit there - people talking.

My father came from Europe.

Now I'm leaving.

Landing in France. There are big ships. We're unloading bags and big boxes. Two or three friends are still with me.

We're sent all over the place. March, stop and do stuff, party. We're in large cities. I'm a Private. No fighting yet.

I'm in a big tent. There are lots of beds. I'm talking. It's an old tent and it smells. I'm talking about having to move to the border. Not to the front, but to west Germany.

Now I'm moving. Carry my stuff - gun, backpack. Walk. Trucks go slow because we're going over mountains.

Still going over mountains but we're a lot closer now.

There are a lot of people at the bottom of a hill. They're very bad people. They don't have guns, but they're yelling at us. They're farmers who don't want us to move over their land.

We've stopped. We must be there. I'm sitting there in camp, reading a magazine. It's a crossword puzzle thing; I get occasional mail.

I'm sick! I have diarrhea and I'm throwing up. A few others are, too. We're in a sick bay thing.

I'm almost better. We're moving again, marching. No one knows where we're going; feels like we've been marching for years. I'm not really comfortable even though I've got good boots.

The Whiteness

&

"I'm A Stud Everywhere"

What does the gold band on your left ring finger mean?

It's a Band of Adversity. It means
I've lived through some hard stuff
and should now be honored.

Are there other architectural structures by the Cathedral?

There are weird-looking buildings on
the side.

There are the lights.

And huge, rocky, mountains.

And just space and the end of space-as-
we-know-it.

You mentioned a castle before.

The little castles, the fortress things, they
house souls.

Who told you of the term, "The Continuum"?

I just knew.

What are the Glastonbury Places?

They're big, very big; some are as big as planets, some as small as a marble. They're for helping lost souls find their way.

They're not conscious; they're just objects. They're stationary and emit energy which can be seen a long ways but not long enough to be seen here. They are brighter than the sun, but you can look at them.

There's a timescape. Some beings use energy to travel it. I never talked to them; just know of them. They can enter and leave where the energy meets, in the Glastonbury Places. They can go through there.

Please explain the Whiteness.

The Whiteness isn't just what we experience directly after death. It's inside of everyone and we can meet there.

It is everything or nothing and we can change it.

Our energy is part of the Whiteness.

All of the Whiteness has energy in it and you can go there and control it.

You can make the Whiteness into a ten-ton ball of light around you or into a jungle.

You can control people, but only bad ones do this. They can control a person even if they've been good.

Also, there are dead ones wanting to experience life again.

In the Whiteness there's someone who may be able to help them, to go to them, or wait for them where they're going when they're dead.

Please explain the levels of beings.

There are souls and there are gods, or rulers, who watch over souls.

Souls.

Demons.

Rulers.

Gods.

Energy.

Thoughts.

Emotions.

There are ranks of beings but no one's better then anyone else.

All are equal.

They all pay for what they've done.

We all have the same abilities unless otherwise taught.

We are good but we can be taught to be evil.

People who have bad souls, they transmit energy which attracts demons and bad energy.

By being good they can change; by becoming spiritual and by doing good deeds.

Beings, people and demons, have souls because they're aware. All other life forms are below.

Most are more self-aware than humans, because they're more conscious of their mistakes.

We're foolhardy; we make mistakes. We can change these.

All souls are connected.

No soul is better than another.

What's a typical angel party like?

The typical party is meeting other souls.

Me and Abe Lincoln could tap the keg; Tahil could party with Jefferson Davis.

It's hanging out with other souls.

Angels can eat and have sex but they don't have to.

They're not monogamous although they may have someone special.

I'm a stud everywhere.

What about ghosts?

They're souls that can't rest yet because they still have stuff to do before they can enjoy it.

They have to go back and say they're sorry and what butt-holes they were; that they didn't mean it, or it was an accident, for their extremes.

But they don't go to Hell.

Hell is for much worse. There are demons everywhere.

There are loved ones to help the dead. Things aren't planned but they're known; all is connected.

So, what are demons?

They are confused souls that take energy from souls of other people and use it in wrong ways.

They can be people but they don't because they can get energy without having to live.

Demons are kind of like outcasts.

They can party down with aliens; they can take whatever form they want.

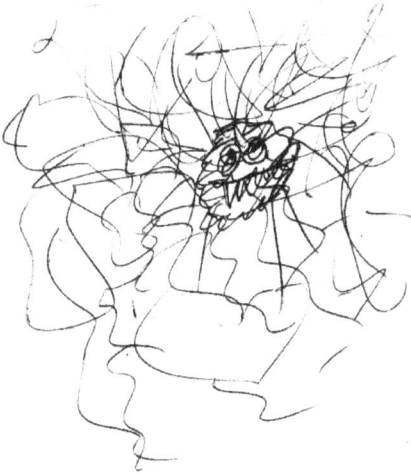

ENERGY, I LIKE BOLTS,
UNTAMED, COMING OFF.
DEMONS ARE KIND of
GOOFY LOOKING.

Demons don't pick up energy until way after death.

What was your first incarnation?

It was as an object.

I stayed in one place a lot.

Describe your favorite planet.

It has different colors, sounds; there are many other beings there, and they're friendly.

Have you come across any famous dead people?

Many, but they're not famous there.

Everyone has been famous, if they want.

How many incarnations have you had and on how many planets?

1,078.

That's just one millionth of my existences.

I've had many lives, role-playing, on almost every planet.

How many incarnations have been on Earth?

I've had 5-600 on Earth. I don't like the planet but I like existing here. I get a lot more attention from everyone; it's less lonely here.

What are angels?

They help souls get wherever; do odd jobs.

Do they all incarnate as humans?

> Some have been human, some not. You
> have the choice unless you're a slouch.

Are there angels who never incarnate?

> No. After a while life is like a vacation
> and you want to take one.

> Only some of us are angels. Can't tell
> who's embodied that's an angel.

> There are plenty of them here taking
> vacations.

*How did you determine to be here this
incarnation? Not why, but how.*

> You have to really want it.

> If you're concentrating and wanting it
> you won't notice when it happens.

Why did you choose me as your mother?

> I didn't really choose you as my mother.
> I must have felt it would be good, on an
> unconscious level. You make the choice
> only you don't notice it; it's just a good
> feeling.

Who built the Cathedral and why?

No one builds things; they're just there.
You have to believe; there's no disbelief.

Well, is it real then?

It's real, but just not physical.

Why don't you go to classes instead of working?

Makes me feel better to make other's lives better.

Have you met Jesus, Buddha, or Mohammed?

Nope.

Please explain the Whiteness again.

It exists in everyone.

It's everything and nothing.

It's not physical.

It's yours and mine.

It's whatever you can imagine.

The light is their soul, so when the Light is a place you have to find it in yourself before you can find it.

So when you're helping someone to find the Light you're helping them to remember.

"Experience the Whiteness again, please."

Once you remember and believe, it's accessible.

"Do you remember this rock, or some planet?"

Like, for an American with amnesia you'd show him the White House.

Are demons more self-aware than humans?

No, not really. They don't realize what they're doing. They're adolescent spirits fighting back without good reason. To them, destruction and anarchy are okay.

Inside the Cathedral
&
The End Time

Please, tell me some more about your favorite planet.

It's a big, purple planet. There's cool stuff on it. It has big, different animals that are nice, unlike other planets. It's squishy, bouncy, rock hard, and sticky in spots. I play here.

What is your favorite state of being?

When I make myself hop and float through asteroid belts, through space, like I'm ruler of everything. The sun might burn me if I accidentally touch it; then I'd be mad and kick it.

Please, tell me more about the Cathedral.

If you had a telescope and you didn't believe, you wouldn't see it.

But it's there; you just have to unlock it, your belief.

It's a place for souls to come through, to and from Hell and other places, and between lives, too.

They go there just to see the Cathedral, too.

First time, when I started there a long, long time ago, there was Nothingness. Then a little warm light flew out of the Glastonbury Light and I was born. I thought, "What's happening?"

I just started all of a sudden. I wanted to be, even without thoughts and existence. Something decided I would be.

The Cathedral was there before I was. The first being built it, is my guess.

Does it look like a Christian cathedral?

It's not really Christian looking. It's just that it looks however you need it.

It's only a place in your mind; it exists in you, in all minds.

Inside there's huge stained glass, so huge! Like never-ending, yet outside it's small.

Is there anything like a cross inside?

No cross, only in my head there's a weird symbol filled with dark red shimmery light. It has curves and shapes in it, like a messed up cross.

Is there anyone inside the Cathedral?

There's probably someone a long ways down.

There are traces of everyone, but no one's really in it. There are aura trails.

You crossed through it, but not up and down.

There are side rooms, chapels, zillions of them. There are little stone closets. They can't be opened. Just the big altars can.

This room has no color.

Only, behind me there's strange tile, and a small, tiny, secret passage with something like an oven door. Then there's a long hall with many windows. There's color here: blue, brown, and white.

Imagine a straight line, now half an oval below it, like a drooping tongue with an "X" like it's crenellated.

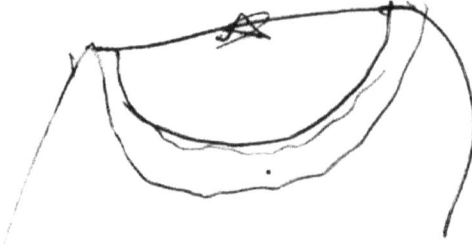

There are a whole bunch of gray clouds; it's a purple, orange, yellow and gray sky.

You can look through the windows; looks like a castle. Sky surrounds it.

Where are you?

I'm just in a hallway; there's no bottom or top. There's just a yellow, purple, orange, red sky.

It opens up to a big courtyard. The center has a risen cylinder with a crenellated castle top.

I feel the presence of other souls but I can't see anyone.

I started another life here. This one, the trail stops here. That life perished there. This trail may be hard to find when I die.

One trail stops here, will end up there, and yet it'll act as though it's not been interrupted.

I'm still there metaphysically but here physically.

I may have been sent to stop the Pope from falling and breaking a finger; it's no matter if I don't succeed. But if I were sent to stop a bullet and I didn't, then I'd lose respect.

Tell me something important.

The end of this Earth's civilization will be 260 some years from now.

How?

How? A third World War or something like that. It will start in Europe; some countries will feud and they'll kill everything.

Only a few folks will be left. And they'll still kill each other. Even over here, in America.

It'll happen not very long after us.

This already happened once, a long time ago. Life faded away; higher forms died out.

What will happen to life on Earth?

Giraffes don't fight so they die a long time after us.

I probably will be here for the End Time.

Why?

Just because I want to.

Will you know the "End Time Signs"?

I'll know them and I'll get here.

It's not coming too soon, 2106 or 2150. Don't know exactly.

Do other planet's endings interest you?

No, not really. They don't have this large a population on them.

We're going to know about it before it happens. We'll rape! Riot! Pillage! Plunder! And rage!!!!

What will the End Time be like?

There will be folks on ships because the land's so bad.

A U.S. ship is cruising to look for good land, a good place to live. There are LOTS of folks on this ship.

It's not as bad as in the movie, "Waterworld"; the land is messed up, but it's not completely gone.

What will happen to them?

They never find it.

The ship gets blown up.

There are six people left on Earth but now there's no land, so they die out.

Sea mammals will live on but no humans will survive.

Eventually all but small things will die out and evolution will start over again. It'll take a long, long, time.

In some places this is a normal pattern.

Tell me about your robe color and what it means.

> Your robe color is your aura color or how bad you've been. White is great. Red is horrible. There are quite a few reds and eventually they'll be dealt with by those with authority.

Who are these beings in authority?

> They are not really beings like people; they're kind of like energy.

What's the meaning of life?

> This life has no meaning; we give it meaning, and that's how we find it eventually.
>
> Life is a vacation!

That's wonderful! Tell me more about your life in space.

> Dick exists on his own.
>
> He's a body with feelings and emotions out in space.
>
> I left him in a remote place and I doubt anyone will find him. He's not activated.

You know how it is, you buy a new one but it's not just right.

Well, what if you can't find him?

If I die and I didn't find Dick's aura trail, I'd start another trail to look for him. But during that time I'd be somebody else.

That's how I was Thomas.

It's like a favorite purple shirt and you move 1,000 miles away but you've forgotten it.

Please, tell me more about the trails.

There's brilliant red, shining glass and there's something like a golf ball, white with a speckled center, and something like a trophy before the glass.

The rooms next to it are pain (on the left) and war (on the right).

This one is niceness because it's really cool.

My trail almost hurt my eyes because I've been here so often.

I stepped in!

I'm in a field with apple trees. Everywhere there's beautiful flowers and grass.

I'm alone right now.

I see my trail on a mountain, about 5-10 miles away.

Oh! To see everything again!

I'm smelling the flowers! I breathe in color! Such a beautiful sweet scent!

I just want to lie down in the flowers and sleep.

These are just my trails here. All mine.

It's great! There are so many different flowers, bushes, grass.

I'm smelling them all. Ah!

This is the most peaceful place I've ever been.

It's my secret place.

It must only be inside me, but it's real.

Maybe it's just mine or I'm the only one who knows about it.

What is this place?

There are trillions of side chapels in the Cathedral. That white golf ball sucked me into one as I was looking at the trophy. Not all the rooms have been explored.

The trails are created through thought. Maybe the rooms represent souls and you can visit them?

This one is mine because it leads to me. Up the stairs, after the stalls, leads me right into me.

(He keeps smelling the flowers, sniffing.)

This place is huge.

There's a mountain range but it's not steep. It's covered in trails, and trees, and flowers; all trimmed and nice.

Everything has a distinct smell.

Wait a minute. What just happened?

That dimpled ball, the centerpiece on a mantel in the stained glass place, it senses and focuses energy. It activates the stained glass; it sucks you in.

The stained glass with the flowers is my special place.

Emotions are focused energy on a subject.

All religious artifacts in church have one meaning: they focus your energy and send it to a higher being. Virgin Mary statues, pictures of Christ and Baby Jesus; all of them.

What about the cross?

The cross is like a crossroads and energy comes in and meets at the center.

This is one of my answers for spiritual consciousness: that focused energy can cause such a channel that pure raw energy can come into you. Old religious fanatics were very focused.

Watch how much energy you can put into prayer! It will bug someone. Like, if you want a red pony and you don't

think about it too much - that kid's not
going to get a red pony.

Thoughts and emotions equal focused
energy.

The difference is doing it and getting it -
getting out and doing it - or focusing
energy on one thing and bugging the
piss out of someone "upstairs".

*How did other peoples figure out how to open
up their brains and use all of it?*

They accepted the Others. The Others
can teach us.

That's why they're hesitant. Other
planets saw them and were friendly to
them.

What clues do we have?

Some of us are psychic; in some of us
there are little clues. There's more to
believe.

It's worked on some people but now the
rest have to believe.

What is the energy you talk of that demons take away from the living?

There's one energy only.

Were demons once alive?

Yeah. They're bad souls.

They're supposed to go to Hell but didn't. Maybe they're not ready yet. Now they're causing mischief and they'll pay for it later.

No one watches over them.

Are there Beings other than Energy Beings who never live?

Thoughts aren't living; they're not really alive, except in your head.

Are you always in a body?

Of course not! You can imagine yourself as anything.

Dick's body is a construct.

When you're floating around on different planets you can take shape; your soul builds an "exoskeleton". It's like a white light kind of body, like the Silver Surfer from "X-Men" but white.

You can touch stuff and feel. But if you get hit it won't hurt, because it's just energy.

You can see Visitors here if you believe. That's why I see things; because I know they're there.

I'm a happier person because I know there's more.

Some people just go from life to life, making their existence a vacation all the time. They either had a bad experience or they like living so much they're almost always in a body. Only when they're making the transition are they out of body.

You once said demons are more self-aware than humans; then again, you also said they're only adolescents and not aware.

Sometimes demons get the wrong idea. They have short attention spans. So you can't talk with them; they'll scream at you or float away or break something.

Do aliens really party down with demons?

Demons are famous for being mischievous and party animals. Anyone can party down with them.

How can a feeling be a Lord?

The feelings inside your head can be alive. One can be hate, one love.

Lords don't have time to have a real life. They're busy watching over everyone else, so any feelings they get they dwell on. They like feelings.

You said that red-robed beings will be dealt with by authorities eventually. How?

The Rulers are like authorities; they make you feel guilty.

No force is used.

The Rulers, or Lords, who dwell on feelings because they don't have time for their own, they're always watching everybody else. They watch over souls.

They just say, "You know where you should be, you shouldn't be here, etc."

Have you met one?

I was just hanging out with my friends on this orange planet.

He slowly floated up to us and I thought, "Oh, no", and he told me, "You should not be here, you should be over there" and you can't ignore him because he stares at you.

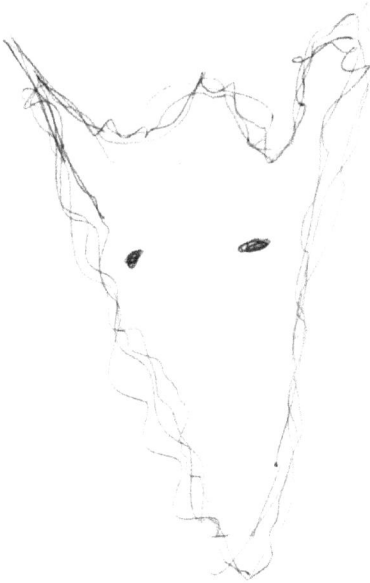

It was a big old purple thing, oddly shaped like South America except the upper left part is just a sharp tip. It's made out of something like hard plastic.

So we left.

I was skipping my job. We were on an orange planet.

 There was an old wooden shack and not enough chairs so I was standing. It was like an old bar with souls inside (not living).

It said, "Why aren't you doing your job? Why are you making someone else do it? You should be on that purple planet."

I've seen other ones, just they didn't talk to me.

Some are black, some are transparent but you can still see them; whatever is their personal preference. Like "Slimer", from "Ghost Busters", the little green monster; like him except larger and transparent.

The black one was weirdly shaped, like if you threw up on a linoleum floor, but he was in a ball. He was very weird looking.

St. Peter Dude,
The Trip to Hell
&
The Cherry Pies

*T*he following is a transcription of a very fortunate recording I made of a session. Unfortunately, it begins mid-sentence:

...and eventually he'll die and then he'll come back and he'll be nine again and he'll grow on. And then, let's say, you'll have another life at fourteen and then you'll die and have another life...

Only up to forty-one? You don't think that Dick will get any older?

Well, he doesn't age. But, I mean...

But others do; that nine year old did.

They age until they're forty-one.

And that's it?

Well, I mean, not everyone! Some people can only have an age of thirty-six; some may have an age of three. But they're the same intelligence level. The three year old can know everything the forty-one year old one's going to know.

Oh, so it doesn't limit your intellectual capabilities, or your spiritual...

Just your size.

Just your size.

And your body, yes.

So, you don't get old?

Nope.

So, there are no old angels?

Well, some of them age up to like 70, 69 or 70. But that's it. Then they live forever.

No angel ever dies.

They just take vacations?

Yes.

Let's go to your first day on the job as Dick. What are you doing?

I'm in a large place. It says "Registration".

Describe it.

There's a lot of wood and there's a lot of people that have those kinds of hats on like the bankers wear – visors! And

tuxedos and crap and they got
mustaches.

They say go here, go there, sign this,
sign that. Blah blah blah. Blah blah blah.
Blah blah blah.

And then they say, "Congratulations!"

And then, what's his name, St. Peter
Dude says, "OK, here's where you go for
today or forever how long, a year or ten
years, to help this person. You go to this
area and help this person; then go to
this area and help this person; and then
you just watch after this person for three
hours" or something like that.

It tells you your whole itinerary at once?

Yup. You have a major capacity in your
brain so you can remember it all.

*Okay, what is Dick doing now, after he's talked
to Saint Peter "Dude"?*

After Saint Peter "Dude"? He flies off to
that place.

How does he fly? Head first? On his back?

He can do it any way.

Some angels have wings and some don't. Some can fly like Superman but they don't need the cape.

Oh. Why do some have wings and some don't?

Some can't even fly.

They can't even fly?

Nope. They have to teleport, you know.

Flying is better.

Why is it better?

It's more fun, plus you get to see a lot more.

Why do some get to and some don't?

Some just can't.

How do they get to learn to get to do it?

You don't get to learn to do it. It's automatic. If you can't, you can't! And then you have to teleport.

You're just lucky that you get to fly?

Yup.

There's nothing you did to earn it?

Nope and I don't have a … ah, let's hold
on a second… they don't balance… but
I don't have to use them, they don't
have to flap for carrying around.
They're just there for looks, saying I'm
the best angel around, blah de blah de
blah.

Oh , really? Because you have wings?

Yup.

So, it has nothing to do with earning wings?

Nope. If they're there, they're there—if
they're not, they're not. Oh, well! Then
you weren't chosen to have a pair of
wings.

*So someone chose you to have wings. Is it
because of your job?*

Yes, mostly.

I mean, a lot of carriers of souls do have
wings and can fly, some don't have

wings and can fly, and some have to teleport.

See, it's mostly the angels around God that have wings and the angels who take people, who take their souls up to Heaven, have the wings.

But if you're lucky, and have another job, you might have wings.

Ah, but it depends upon your job?

Yes; depends upon the kind of job you have.

Who chooses? Does Saint Peter choose your job?

Well, if Saint Peter's too busy then God will. If Saint Peter doesn't have the time then another angel will, or sometimes you can.

You say, "I'd like to be this" and they say, "Okay, we've got room for this," and you can do it

I had to go to Hell once, if you want to talk about it.

What was that like?

Not cool.

Describe it, please.

It's not hot down there, but everything's red and looks like it's hot, but it's not. There's a lot of snakes; they come out of the walls, out of the rocks.

There are a lot of illusions that scare you.

There are cliffs, a lot of pits, and there's a lot of scary stuff. And there's a lot of ghosts down there, a lot of bad ghosts.

How come you went there?

I had to run an errand for God. I had to go down there and take a scroll.

Really! Did you read the scroll or did you know what it was about?

I'm not allowed; nobody's allowed. Not even Saint Peter "Dude" is allowed to read God's stuff.

So, God has correspondence?

What do you mean "correspondence"?

He has to write things down, he just doesn't think things to ... to down there?

He can but it's more official using other people.

Are messages often relayed?

Yes.

So, who did you give the message to?

I gave it to kind of like the Devil's secretary.

What did they look like?

It's a she.

What did she look like?

She wore a grey dress and all this stuff but she was red.

What kind of dress?

It's like a grey businesswoman's dress suit and pink blouse. She didn't have horns or anything like that. But her body was red.

Was she pretty?

I guess so; you could say that.

Do you know why she's down here?

I wouldn't know. You don't want to really talk to them because they're not very nice.

So, you just hand it over?

I just said, "This is from God."

How did you have protection when you went there?

God said, "You are protected; nothing can hurt you."

Oh, so you got it straight from God's hands?

Uh huh. And that's when I got to meet God.

Oh, so what was God like?

His voice sounded like a man's.

Why? Because it was deep, or…?

It was deep and like a man's voice, kind
of like Mr. Richards' voice.
[Mr. Richards was one of our neighbors,
with a deep voice.]

From a big body?

Yeah.

*Okay. So, describe it. How did you know you
were to go see God? Who told you?*

Saint Peter said, "This is where you walk
up these stairs; God has something for
you to do." Oh, cool! Kind of like the

inner royal what-ever-you-want-to-call-it …Heaven.

So you walked up the stairs? Why didn't you fly?

It's more respectful to walk.

But if you need to get somewhere really quick they have little highways, like ribbons, that show the way to go. Like, exit this way to a mountain scene, this way to Registration Office, this way to restaurants and shopping, and golf.

You mean there's shopping there?

I mean it's like… you can imagine it. You can say, okay, I want to play some golf now and right in front of you –

It's endless all of it, so every person has enough room for miles and miles…

Of … whatever you imagine?

Yeah, see…

Or, whatever you want?

You can do whatever you want. You can say, okay, I want to play some put-put now or you can say I want to go to the driving range now. I want to drive a car around… but you can't hurt anybody with a car because it's not really there. It's just like it is…

Can you feel it?

Well, yeah, to you it's real. But a person might go right through the car if you try to hit them because it's not really there. It feels like it is to you because you're imagining it.

What about food?

You can get the satisfaction but you won't gain any weight.

What about smoking?

You can still smoke, too. It's unlimited.

So, you got to be an errand person?

No, I mean, I think there are others like me but let's say everybody's busy in that one department and the errand boy will say, "Okay, take this to the janitorial area," and then I'll just take that there and go back and then he'll say, "Okay, now go pick this person up; he's from the planet Zorkel," and I'll fly down there.

Do you have a regular work schedule? Do you start at a certain time and quit at a certain time?

No. At any time I can stop work. I don't get paid or anything. I could not work at all since there are so many of us. I mean, nobody could work at all and the job would still get done.

The job will still get done even if you don't work?

Yes.

So, there are many angels who are assigned the same task?

> Oh, yes, there are millions and millions and millions. But there are only certain ones in certain areas. It's all so huge.

So, what's your area?

> My area's Sector HR... sometimes Z... Sector something... Oh, there's Sector 11181167HZYQ, something like that. But that's just a part, like a little country.

How many parts and countries are there?

> Oh, man! They're endless, endless, endless; so many. So many, so many, so many.

But God's Staircase is everywhere?

> Oh, no, you can just take the highway. Angels with wings automatically earn the teleport when they need it so they can just say, "Teleport me to God's Staircase right at this moment."

And you'll be right there. But you have
to have Saint Peter's permission to go
up there.

*So, teleporting is even more of a privilege than
having wings?*

Oh, everyone has teleport. But wings are
only for certain jobs, let's say.

What's been your worst job?

Rescuing a soul in a bathroom.

I remember this one guy, someone who
died while in a bathroom, an old man,
on Earth, in an apartment building in
Chicago.

He had trouble leaving. He didn't want

75

to. He was afraid of leaving.

I told him it would be all right and eventually he came. It took twenty minutes! "You remember the Whiteness, don't you?"

He wasn't his old self, so he remembered, but he still wanted to stay with his family in his home.

"It's not your time here and you're no longer a part of it here."

I got kind of angry at him.

Who told you to go there?

I was told at a desk to go there. A woman, the kind of old lady who'd bake you cookies and you could call her Grandma, told me. Her name was Fanny.

She often tells me where to go and what to do. She's kind of like Saint Peter. There is no Saint Peter; just plenty of people who are like our idea of him. They know everything about you and if you're a good person.

She'll tell you where the fun stuff is and she'll tell the bad people not to go there, to go elsewhere during that time. Every bad person has a chance but they wreck things for everyone.

Are you happy?

Oh, yeah. Oh, yeah.

Do you have friends?

Oh, yeah. Everybody's there.

Who's your best friend?

Everybody! Everybody there is your best friend.

Can you tell what people are thinking or do you talk? Can you tell what other angels are thinking or do they talk?

Oh, they talk! Only some people can read minds. Like, you wouldn't call them generals; they're just those who are in charge. They'll say, "Don't think about that, you can't think about that while you're working!"

Really? There's thought control?

Oh, no, it's not really thought control. I mean, they can't stop you from thinking that, but they'll say, "Please don't, it takes your mind off your work." Then you'll say, "Oh, well", and then I'll go think about it while I eat or something. You can go eat and take as long as you want.

So that's how you take care of unwanted thoughts? Or unproductive thoughts?

Uh hmmm.

Oh! And you don't have to eat there. You get automatically nourished.

But you might want to eat?

Yeah, just to have that nice feeling, that satisfaction from eating.

Who cooks?

The food's just there.

What if you wanted to cook?

Then you could say, "Take me to a kitchen, with this, this and this there in the refrigerator and I'd like to make this and this," for however many you want to cook for.

Are there parties? Do you give parties?

Yeah, everybody has a party.

You'll just say, "I'd like to invite (you'll just pick randomly) like, this, this, this and this person," and then some will say "Ooh, I'm sorry but I'm playing golf at that time", "Ooh, okay, I can come", "Ooh, okay I know this person – I can come"; like that. Like, everybody you know.

So, everybody you know is there, eh?

Uh, huh. Only you don't even have to send out invitations or tell them. They'll just automatically know. They'll know. They'll say, "This and this person's having a party tonight." "I know it!" Automatically.

Hold on a second.

Everybody has a little bit of mind control. They can say [in a voice like a hypnotist's], "Come to my party." And the other person will say, "Oh, they're having a party tonight!"

Is there anyone that you miss, that isn't there that you've known?

No. No. If there's anybody that you like they'll probably be there anyways.

What if you like somebody that went to Hell?

You can visit them. They have special visiting hours in special places that aren't so bad.

Can you still communicate with people in Hell?

Oh, yeah. Those that are better at mind control, you can say, "Hi, Bob. How are you?" And that person will say, "Oh, he's talking to me" and then he'll automatically think, "Hi, Bob, how are you?" and then he'll go, "Oh! I'm fine. Blah blah blah." Like that.

So, why do people think it's so bad to go to Hell?

Well, they did bad things in their last life. Let's say they raped somebody or shot somebody. Then they might only have to serve 5 years and then they'll get to go up to Heaven.

So, it's like prison or jail?

Yeah.

So, how do they get better there?

How do they get better?

Yes, what improves them?

Oh! And, um, if you're down there for eternity you don't get a vacation.

Who would be down there for eternity?

Oh, let's say Al Capone or Columbus or whatever.

Why Columbus?

Because he skinned up all those Indians.

So, that would earn him instant eternity in Hell?

No, not eternity. Let's say maybe 50,000 years.

Oh. That's a pretty long time, isn't it?

Yeah.

So do they have schools down there to teach them to be better or do they just make them go through pain or is it…?

No, there's not really pain; they don't chain them up and hit them with whips or anything but it's very boring down there, there's <u>nothing</u> to do, and then they'll think, "Oh, my God, in my next life I'm going to be good because then I get to go to Heaven and do whatever I want."

Do they remember that in their next life?

Uh huh. They'll feel really guilty whenever they do anything bad; they'll learn not to do it.

Uh huh, so guilt is a remembrance.

I went to Hell some, one time or another. Everybody has.

Oh. That's how we know about it?

Yup. Every life you'll go to Hell after

some time for like maybe one day, one month, one year for whatever you did.

Who's in charge down there? Is it "down"? Why do we think it's "down" there?

Well, because it's almost like underground. There's no sky down there. Everything is red. It's like a huge red tunnel. It's like pillars, no, not like pillars—I mean it's all stone. There's a lot of dirt and it's red.

Is there bubbling stuff there?

That's what I was just thinking about! That's their water. It's very hot so it's hard to drink. It doesn't cool down really, so you can still drink the water, but it teaches you that Hell is bad.

Oh, and if they're good that one year they will get to play golf or whatever and they'll say, "Okay, I'd like to play 18 rounds for my present this year."

Do they get presents?

Well, if they're good! Let's say if somebody's really bad forever and they're like beating up people down there then they don't get any gift.

Oh, so there's still stuff they can do down there?

There are rewards.

They can interact with other people?

Uh huh. I mean there are so many people down there they invented games anyways. They play stone ball.

So, let's go back to the time you've been there.

Uh, nobody remembers that time because it's either too bad to remember or you don't want to remember. On the way up to Saint Peter you'll say, "Please tell God that so and so and so, number -- ---- would like to not remember his experience in Hell starting -----."

Ohhhh, well, that's interesting.

They blank that out.

So, does everybody have a number?

Oh, it's sort of like your social security number or zip code.

So, does everyone in the universe, the multi-universe, have one?

Uh huh.

Are there more dimensions than one?

Endless, there are so many. It's not endless, I mean, but there must be zillions.

Wow. Do they all have their own Heavens and Hells?

No, it's just one huge Heaven.

So, you get to meet beings from other dimensions there?

Yes.

Do we form friendships and then come back and kind of know them in-between dimensions so that you could have a friend in another dimension right now?

Yeah, I could. But, I do, probably, and I'll get to see him next lifetime or whenever.

Do you think you communicate now, in any way?

Um, probably in my dreams. When you're in life dreams are a way of communicating.

With...?

With anybody!

Let's say, you have a dream about a nice big mountain and a river and all this other stuff and you catch a nice big fish. Well, that fish can be your friend from another thing and you somehow communicate with him. That could be your friend in a dream. Everybody connects through dreams.

So, is the fish a symbol?

No, not a symbol. Your friend's sleeping and he's in that dream.

And he's the fish being caught?

Did you ever dream you're walking down a street and there's a whole bunch of people there? There's a whole bunch of people in one place or you're in a

game show and there's an audience?
Those are all the people sleeping.

*Oh. All the other people in your dream are
people sleeping?*

Uh huh.

*Are there people we don't know in our
dreams?*

Oh, yes.

They don't appear familiar.

No, they don't appear familiar but after
a while you may get to know them in
your dreams. But you won't remember
them while you're awake. In your
dreams they'll go, "Happy!"

So, you get to know them in your dreams?

Yes.

So, you have dream friendships?

Uh huh, and then while you're in
Heaven or Hell you might meet that
friend there. Or as a special present in
Hell you can say, "I'd like to be
connected with this and this person for

a day," but in Heaven, if that person's there, you can just say, "I'd like to see blah-blah-blah now!" and you'll just magically appear where that person is.

So, when you're in Heaven you can keep in touch with the people you left back on Earth?

Yeah. I mean, they can't see you but they'll know your presence. Like maybe that thing right there may be an angel just trying to say, "Hi!"

What thing?

That flasher thing, because maybe it's just an angel that's come down. It's there and it just wants to see me for a while.

Huh! Even though it's the tape recorder that's flashing saying that it's a voice recording that's going on? Whenever you make a sound, the red light flashes.

Where?

On this tape machine.

Oh.

Is that the light you were talking about?

No.

Oh. What light are you talking about?

The flasher – you know.

Oh! The flasher here in the house! [We'd repeatedly had something that appeared to be a ball of colored light flashing inside the house around the bathroom/library area.]

Yeah – that could be an angel that's trying to visit me, one of my friends that just got back to Heaven or Hell or wherever.

Is there some way you can know about that right now? You can know for sure?

No, there's nothing you can know for sure. I can say, maybe when I die in 50 years, whenever, or 70, and then I'll go up there and I'll say, "Hey! When I was 13 did you come down and visit me?" And they'll say, "Oh, yeah! I did!" or maybe, "No, I wasn't there."

Okay, so, how many in-between-lifetimes have you lived as Dick?

In-between? Oh, every one.

Every one? You always go back to being Dick?

Oh, you can say, I'll always be me,
myself, but I'll say, "Well, today as Dick
I'd like to be a woman, blah blah blah."

*What? Dick can choose who he wants to be
every day?*

Yeah, you can say, "I'd like my figure to
be a woman with big breasts."

*Hmm! So, that's sort of like another illusion?
Your body is an illusion?*

Yeah. And you can't get hurt either.
Can't get burned; nothing can happen
to your body.

Can you have sex?

Yeah.

Can you have children?

Mmm, yes, you can, but you never have
a real partner.

You never have a real partner?

No, I mean, yeah, you do, but there's just no such thing as marriage up there.

Because you love so many?

Uh huh.

That's nice. Let's see…what else can I ask?

Oh, there are many questions.

Okay, how about if you just… just start talking?

Okay.

I've been to a lot of planets but I haven't been…I've only been to one millionth of all the planets there are.

Wow!

Yup. And, ah, I've been to maybe a thousand, five thousand, ten thousand, I'd say about, maybe, oh, one million planets I've been to.

You know exactly how many planets; how many planets have you been to?

976,841 planets.

Wow. Why did you go there?

To get souls.

Are there some souls who are more at ease with dying?

Yes.

Which ones are these?

The ones that <u>know</u> the time they're going to die, when they're going to die.

How do they know?

They'll just, like, have it printed on their hand; it'll say when they're born, Exordiazobziggy 1- that'll be the date that they'll die.

So it's preordained? It's preplanned?

Uh huh.

So who planned it for them; they did?

No. It's just there. Their body automatically shuts down that day, at that time; their body just, "click!" wears out.

That's real planned obsolescence!

Yeah.

Okay, are they humanoid?

Some are; some aren't.

Okay, what are some of the strangest ones you've ever come across? That we would consider strange as humanoids.

I've come across some ones you can't even see they're so small, to ones that are eight hundred million times our size.

Wow. Are there ones that are made out of gas, or ones made out of liquid?

Oh, yes. Every kind of one you can think of.

If you think of one made out of chocolate pudding it's out there.

Haha! Really?

Yeah.

Hahaha! That's interesting.

It is. Or one that looks like a banana. It's out there.

Have you come across these, actually?

Oh, no, but you know they're out there.

Okay. How about some of the ones you've come across <u>actually</u>?

Okay. There's the Cherry Pies.

What are they like?

I like Cherry Pies. They're filled with cherries but they don't taste like it. They've got the crust and something else on them.

And the smell?

They don't smell like them but they look like them. And they've got little legs that are black.

Hmmm!

And they walk around, and they talk by moving.

Oh, my goodness!

So, if one goes like this it could mean, "Hi, how are you?" and if one goes like this it means, "Fuck off, buddy!" or whatever.

They have families?

Yeah.

How long do they live?

Oh, they live… ummm… hold on. I think that… uhhhh…

They live a long time, short time?

Some live a very short time; some very long. Maybe one will live 50 million years and one will live for 5 seconds.

Oh. So what is time like? Does time change?

Time is nothing.

Time is nothing? It just depends upon where you are?

Where you are… (Yawn).

What is our time like compared to other times?

Oh, (yawn) let's see. A year on another planet may be 365 days to us but in human days it could be 8 million days, or a year over there could be 30 seconds, maybe. So that person could only live for maybe 60 minutes.

But, it would seem like a longer life or would it seem short?

It would seem very short or it would seem very long. Then you may go on to a life after that that has 50 million years you get to live.

Okay, so what's the whole purpose of everything?

The whole purpose of everything?

Yeah. What's the purpose of living and then dying and living a different life and then dying and then being something else and then living another life and then dying and then being an angel and then living another life...what's the whole purpose?

What's the whole purpose? Wow.

It started out as - I don't know - I don't think anybody knows. I think God's the only one who knows and he never told us. I mean, I think it started out as something. I mean, everything I've talked about could only be a molecule; I mean just like a part of your hair or something. It could be a whole universe right here.

Hmmm. So, it's very vast?

Uh huh.

And this is only the part that you know?

Uh huh.

Have you been around since the very beginning?

No. I was born out of need. What do

you call it? When you say, "We need an angel for bringing back souls." They'll say, "This angel and this angel have a baby." They'll do it and then a baby will pop out 30 seconds later.

Ooh! So, who were your parents, your angel parents?

Aw, um, well you don't really have a relationship with them because they've had so many other babies. They just say this and this person have this baby.

(End of recording.)

Aura Trails,
Energy Bodies,
&
Demons

re there nasty planets?

Do you mean nasty in themselves?
Or that they have nasty
   inhabitants?

None are really nasty. Some are hot,
muggy, and sticky; just all those things
that make you uncomfortable.

For nasty inhabitants, there are very tall
gold robot men. They're mean and they
possess many planets because they take
them over. They're greedy. They rule
wherever they take over. No one calls
them anything or even talks about them
for fear they'll come and get them.

*Are angels' bodies shared? Like, how you
became Thomas because you couldn't find
Dick's trail.*

You never leave a body behind. The
energy disbands and your soul goes on,
or the body decomposes.

The soul looks like a pair of lungs but
kind of like a heart, too, with little lines
around the inside of the edge when not
in the body. It's made out of white light.

It's kind of like in your body by your lungs but higher, by your shoulders. It's most comfortable there but you can have it elsewhere.

Do souls have individual names?

Souls aren't properly named. They may be known to others by a name, but never given a name.

Tell me more about energy bodies.

When you let the body go, the energy will slowly disband. You die; your soul can wander from where it should go.

If the soul has an energy body it can drop slowly; or if you're flying to another planet it will disband like particles of sand, like something made of wet sand which has dried, and is being blown off---like a trail.

It's very pretty if you get to see it.

Yours was a reddish-purple trail, which is very odd as usually there's no color. Maybe you wanted to leave your body to go into another one or because you visited Djuradj [a root past life of mine, involved in many battles].

There are six stars on the high part of the wall and on the lower there's a half circle of concrete, with six stained glass pictures on the side of pain, death, hangings, and beatings. Your body entered into one stained glass picture of hanging and impaling so you might have gone to see Djuradj.

Djuradj can come see you, too. It depends.

Tell me more about aura trails.

The red-purple aura trail is very rare. It means violence. You've been extremely violent. Maybe that's why you're now as you are [non-violent].

You ended <u>many</u> lives under your orders and your aura is almost solid with blood. It's dripping; it's like a thin film on my fingers from touching the mist of your aura! Although it's not like I could pop a hole in it.

It's a very long aura trail because there's such a huge past. Except at the back of

the Cathedral, where you came out a
window, it's almost orange there.

Like, a serial killer like Ted Bundy has
only killed 30 people but Hitler is more
like your color.

You're working this karma off, but it will take a long time. You've got greed from then, too.

How do you know this?

I have a concrete picture of this and I just know it's there, like déjà vu.

Well, what is an aura trail?

It can be small or 50 miles long.

It tells how old, what experiences, where you're going, and if you stopped. But it depends. Also matters how bright it is.

I can't tell exactly whose it is by looking. It looks like Winston Churchill's trail because of blah blah blah but you can feel their feelings that they've left behind unconsciously. So it's difficult to tell.

Whatever you're conscious of, believe in and like, you take with you. And you dump the bad stuff in your aura trail.

What's the weirdest thing you've seen there?

It was some weirdoes out there who have sex with horses in a jelly factory.

What else?

In the Whiteness I saw a metal box shaking.

I walked up and opened it and there was an old guy masturbating in a box of cigar butts, big ol' stogie butts.

He saw me.

The box was full size. He was scrunched in it.

He looked at me and I closed the lid and locked it. You don't want him out. He can imagine himself out; I just didn't want someone else to have the experience of finding him, like a child or a woman wouldn't find it quite as amusing.

His soul was probably a new one and he'd just died and he wanted to be that old guy and masturbate again.

You once said demons are more self-aware than humans but you also said that they're only adolescents and not aware! Which one is it?

They're not aware of what they're doing. It's like, "I'm breaking something, big deal!"

But they are aware they'll have to pay for it in Hell.

Who's going to make them pay for it?

There are no angel police.

No one can give or receive force.

So, they're partying until they get caught or decide to give up because they're tired of what they're doing. It's like growing up.

Almost everyone's been one. After they go to Hell they go to the Whiteness.

There is no Heaven or Hell. You see it as you believe it.

Nothing in Hell can really hurt you; it just makes you not want to come back.

We've all been there a few times.

People there kind of know when their time is up. If they leave early they'll be there longer next time.

You've talked about cats. What about dogs?

There are things like dogs. Some have horns!

They're not tamed elsewhere.

People don't really have pets or companion animals, just rulership over other animals.

It's different here because, in the early days to survive, humans had to get along with animals.

When was your first trip to Earth?

My first trip to Earth was during the Neanderthal period. I was here living it: clubbed it, skinned it, ate it. That kind of stuff.

Earth was very beautiful with a lot of big mountains and glaciers.

What other kinds of things have you and your friends found out there?

I was cruising and found something cool. It was an old man. I took him all over the place to see his deceased relatives in the Whiteness and then I left him.

He would have been a ghost because he was alone and afraid, trapped in his house.

Most of the time folks can choose to be in the Whiteness. It can be changed to anything.

Most aren't chosen for this kind of work. Maybe every fourth soul is chosen to be an angel and there's an infinity of angels.

All souls are created in the same way.

There are new souls.

And some souls die because they're so tired of everything and there's no energy left and they just fade away.

Some may take 10,000 years to become

in-tune, some only 15.

Tell me some more about the Cathedral.

Well, you can go through the floors.
The floorboards can go anywhere you
want to go, like a transporter. You can't
just use thought to travel on.

There are minor changes in it in
different lives, but for the most part I
see it as a Cathedral.

Can you see your aura trail?

I've already dumped all the bad stuff
from my last life. I must not have been
in a life for a long time because there's
no trail for anyone to follow me.

Is there a devil?

Well, there is an evil being, even more
truculent than I am now!

Tell me some more about how you travel.

I used the pillars to first get up to
Heaven before I knew how to use my
ability to use my own mind and float.

Then, there's also a stairway.

I floated, or flew, down to Hell. The color changes gradually.

There's no ground; you just float through air.

Describe your trip to Hell.

Well, it was pretty cool. I was all messed up and there were bad things around. Like the color you see when you close your eyes, orange-ish red.

Do you ever have any trouble?

Well, from falling in love out there. Everyone has.

I'm always a male up there and rarely ever in a lifetime.

Tell me something interesting.

Humans that have been taken to see if they can survive – some have, some haven't - all over. Some very close.

One was on the moon. It died a few years ago.

They suffocated a baby. The bad ones did this.

What do these "bad ones" look like?

The dark, dark, dark ones; the mean ones.

They can go everywhere.

They like research; they sell it, like spies.

They're only happy during times of war so they can succeed. So they try to create wars. There are a few small ones around here and they're trying to make a big one. Little tiny things happening here but if there should be a big one we should watch out!

What are they called?

People name things, so you expect a name for them – but they're just The Dark Ones.

They have black rubbery skin with sharp insides. They have ribs sticking out. It makes you sick to look at them. You can see wiggly things under their skin.

They're collecting information.

I've felt them around a few times.

They can inflict the most pain of any creature. They can bend you, snap you, melt you. They can melt a hundred people at once.

Whatever side they're on wins.

The Mantis People are like them except they gather research for themselves.

They're Utopians; they make everything perfect.

In short, what's important to know?

There's connection and order, love and guidance, eternity and evolution within the group creation of all realities.

Do you have a question for this angel on vacation?

Nicholai welcomes any questions you would like to ask Dick the Carrier Angel.

Send them to him as an email:

angelonvacation@myfatfox.co.uk

Or send a letter to the publisher:

My Fat Fox Ltd
86 Gladys Dimson House
London E7 9DF
United Kingdom

Selected questions will be answered in *Angel On Vacation: Volume 2.*

www.ingramcontent.com/pod-product-compliance
Lightning Source LLC
LaVergne TN
LVHW011403080426
835511LV00005B/390